Tea of Tibet

Fateme Banishoeib

Tea of Tibet. Copyright © 2015 Fateme Banishoeib

All Rights Reserved. Printed in the United States of America. No part of this book may be used or reproduced in any manner whatsoever without written permission except in the case of brief quotations embodied in critical articles and reviews.

1 2 3 4 5 6 7 8 9 10

ISBN-13: 978-1515127956

To the women who dream:

As children, we are told that dreams help us to live better. As women, we learn dreams make our spirits restless.

Traveling to Tibet was one of those dreams for me. At times walking heavy; at others flying lightly. Traveling far enough to meet ourselves.

Anthony Bourdain said that travel isn't always pretty. It is not, nor comfortable, and it leaves marks in the memory and in the heart. The dream is to leave something good behind. The eyes see beyond the dreams creating an extension of the heart using a pen and a camera.

The magic is making up the journey as we go.

This book collects the desire to explore other cultures, territories and discover what makes all us human. It represents a passion for discovering diversities and it is an invitation to go explore to make life fuller and richer and not to escape life.

To women who dream forever seeking!

A Noi

Journey

Separating the seeds from the dirt
Discriminating
Making the difference
Choosing
Self-determining our intrinsic nature
Without bending to "Sort of"
What do I crave?
What do I desire?
For what do I yearn?
The checkpoints to ourselves
Holding to the inner energy of no cheating
The journey to me
The trip to forget who I became
and remember who I am
Walking
Talking
Under the roof of the world
A vacation from what I am not
That leaves only one me
The one thirsty for illuminate water
pouring from the spring

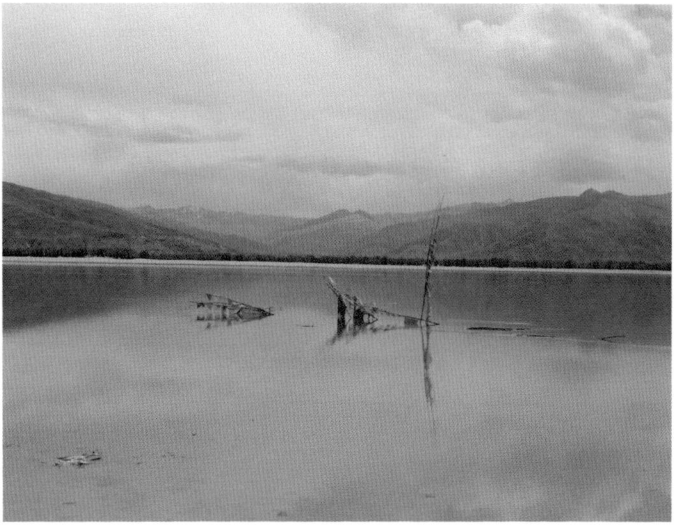

A Prayer

I long to connect with a larger truth
I long to see clearer
So I pray the butter candle to see myself in others
To listen deeply and trust the extraordinary
I pray to see and be seen
I pray for love making moments
I pray to see what my mouth can't speak
I pray to be seen with no misperception
I pray to see when I am alone
I pray to be seen when I stumble
I pray for what I am longing to be seen
I pray for the resurrection after the ego death

Maybe

Maybe a monk
Maybe just a man
Maybe I see you and I can only imagine me
Maybe a guide seeking to learn
Maybe a pure intention
Maybe I do not know who you are
Just fire under the snow
Maybe

Tibet

Beautifully hidden
Beckoning uncertainty
Intricacies of existences
Befriend the enemy
Once a friend maybe
Capable of illusions and magic
Like playing cards on a snowy night under the fire

Two sides of a coin
Spiritual and consumerism
Chosen by what we bring to duality
Dualities and reality
Among demons and deities
The yak butter burning for luminous understanding

The most complex conversation
between ignorance and inner knowledge
One by one everything falls
Unconditionally
Unrequited
Mountains holding up the mirrors of holy waters
Where the fruit of truth plays the game of life
Or survival

The very essence of being on the journey to Nirvana
From here to there
From present to future
Where to care deeply for what we find along the way

Stripped the unnecessary of our desires
Asking for the ultimate letting go

Back Side

Where the apparent order leaves space to reality
Where a woman hangs the working clothes washed
by sweat and soap
Where flags dance with the wind
Where the voices come up unseparated in a day-to-
day conversation
Where the deities watch the flowers blossom
Where a cat hides to find rest
Back side of a life lived full front
The reason we struggle comparing the backside with
the highlight
Where insecurity becomes a messy balcony on the
back side

Go Big or Go Home

Well going it is
Going somewhere
Going to seek
Going to explore
Going to meet
Going to embrace
Going in the dark to see lighter
Is this going big or going home?
It is both
Going big home

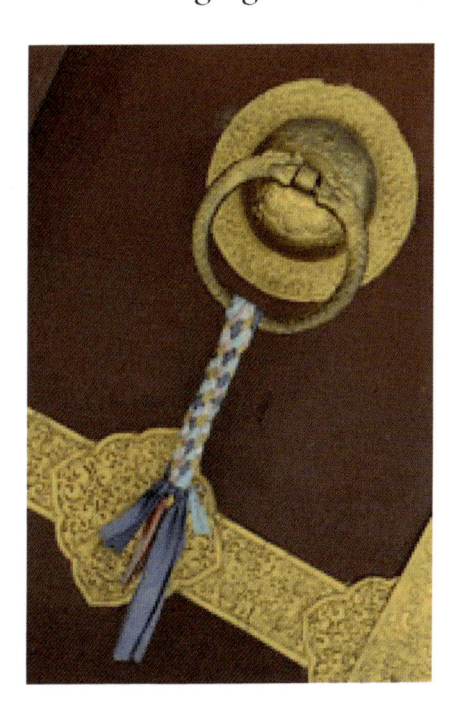

As Old as Mountains

Rising up very clear
Teaching where we are holding back
Constant messengers of where we stuck
Does it get lonely?
The aura of equanimity and dignity covering the pilgrims
I
A city girl
Can't grasp how much is at stake
I need wilderness as they

*"I have nothing new to teach the world.
Truth and Non-violence are as old as the hills.
All I have done is to try experiments in both on as vast
a scale as I could." -- Gandhi*

Moneta

Pray Moneta
The goddess of prosperity
The goddess of money
The fairy queen distributes money
By dirty hands
The stewards of the money
Made faithful of the little things
Content of their virtues
Choosing to live frugal
Abandoning the stress
For the pursuit of wealth
Holding loosely
To the gift of creating wealth
Certainly not

Stars

Look up at the stars
Where the sky is closer
Blessing the chaos within
It will give birth to music
The stars will dance
Praying the stars to be lucky to find love
Asking the stars to remind me to dance with Love
every day
The melody playing in my heart
There is no lie in my stars

The Power of Words

Mean what you say
And say what you mean
Words the mirror of what lies within
A word it is you
Your whole story
Everything or nothing?
At times almost a different you speaking
The you that's unknown
The you that remains empty
Unlived
So tempting to use only pretty words
Or popular words readily understood
It takes bravery to say it all
Words you are ashamed of
Words you know are right
It's all part of you
It is your story

Oneness

Up on the roof of the world
Surrounded by walls
Going up and more up
Suddenly the view opens up
To the traveler waking up

From the sleep of altitude sickness
Juxtaposed to the abyss of ignorance
From that dark multitude of objects
The view of a valley

The Yarlung River reflecting sky and earth
So close we can't see it
Like the eye to see its own lashes
Has to get closer to the point of illusion

It's all an illusion

The mind's mirage dissolving in the appearance
Pass after pass
From one valley to another
To the transparent water
being one
with the Sun
with the Sky
with the Earth

Scriptures

Asceting for the pleasure of knowledge
Exploring the burning desire of knowing
Hiding in the forest
'Til the injuries of ignorance are healed
Let me learn freedom
All these dusty books
Rarely opened
Not touched for respect?
They can't heal our minds
As leaving the prescription by the bedside
Does not cure
The heart needs cutting
Hammering
'Til it becomes familiar
'Til off that cushion
Walk the path to death
Offering fruits of love to the earth

Mandala

The simplicity of a circle
The structure for the spirit to become dust
The contemplative art of the spirit
through the human hands
Just matter of chance being born as human
Casted in virtuous labyrinth the path back to spirit
The subjective convoluted into the ideology
of destiny and faith
Wise fingers posing grain after grain
In the attempt to tame the *ipse*
The chance of the discipline to get to the center
Entering the door of vacuity
At the core all the forms dissolve
Like dust in the wind
At the end the infinite node opening up
Disclosing the heart's passions

Emptiness

One by one all of me falling
Dissociation is the drama of the mind
Thank you for the Chaos
The controlled order condemn in the shops of Lhasa
Its death is the symbol of the loss
Chaos lost the confusion and the indistinct
It gained senses to taste sweets in bulk
Good and bad
Sweet and sour
Existing in the subjective invasion
Of the exterior world
into the inner empty world

Blue Sky

Plus loin
Plus haut
Our desires
Travelers
Seekers
Trying to get to the EBC
Our mortal wandering to the blue sky
Ultimately a vision
Rising up to dive into our inner cave
Rediscover another reality
With no choice
There are no objects in the hermit's cave
There is nothing to see

Clarity

Sweet rich offers to the Buddha
Infinitively burning
Begging for light
Into the darkness
Of a stuffed temple
Praying for a vision
Praying for the dissolution of illusion
It takes work to make milk into butter
It takes travelling into the abyss
To gain clarity
The heart's journeys
Seeking empty luminous clarity
Into the darkness

Unicorns

This rainbow bridge
Where the unicorns
Cross the tremulous way
The channel to choices
This end or another side?
I ride the unicorn
With the promise
There will be light on the way
It is time to cross our connection
And honoring that promise

Peaceful

Undisturbed by the turmoil
Quietly going at 10 kilometers per hour
Even if it takes another life to cross the city
Peacefully observing the parade
Coexistence the path of least resistance
Distant resistance that rhymes with persistence
Both
Meditative and passive
Coexist
Contributing to transport the soul
Across the border

Fire

Ceremonies to erase the stories
Of oppression
And uprising
Wipe cleaning the ugly realities
Fire to forge a wedding ring
Beautiful
Unpractical
Fire consumes
Warms
Illuminates
Fire brings pain
Death
The only element
Human can produce and reproduce
The bridge between mortals and gods
Light my fire
To destruct
And regenerate
Before I vanish

Versions of truth

Flesh becoming word
Word becoming flesh
It is not enough just to live
Needing to speak what is lived
Through the word
We internalize
Different versions
Of what makes this experience truly human

Illusions

I shoot
My illusion of transparency
My emotions running high
The truth is
I stand
In front of a mirror
Leaking out thoughts and emotions
Visible to the world
Blindly transparent

Seeds

Thread one by one
Constructed in a repetition of 108 beads
A symbol
A celestial residence for the meditating man
The doorway to the comprehension
of Love
of Compassion
of Joy
of Equanimity
The universe made tangible
We humans do not understand
The seeds of Buddha are not for sale
No trade for the intangible secrets

The unique answer
To the never ending whys
The rebelling mind
In the eternal mandala circle
Continuously asking why
Suddenly
As a quake
He would answer
It's like this
And then smile
Hoping that with the time
We would adjust
Then
Shocked
By the sound of our silences
Still asking

Chains

The eternal knot
Has no beginning no end

Is a spiritual look
At the infinite chains

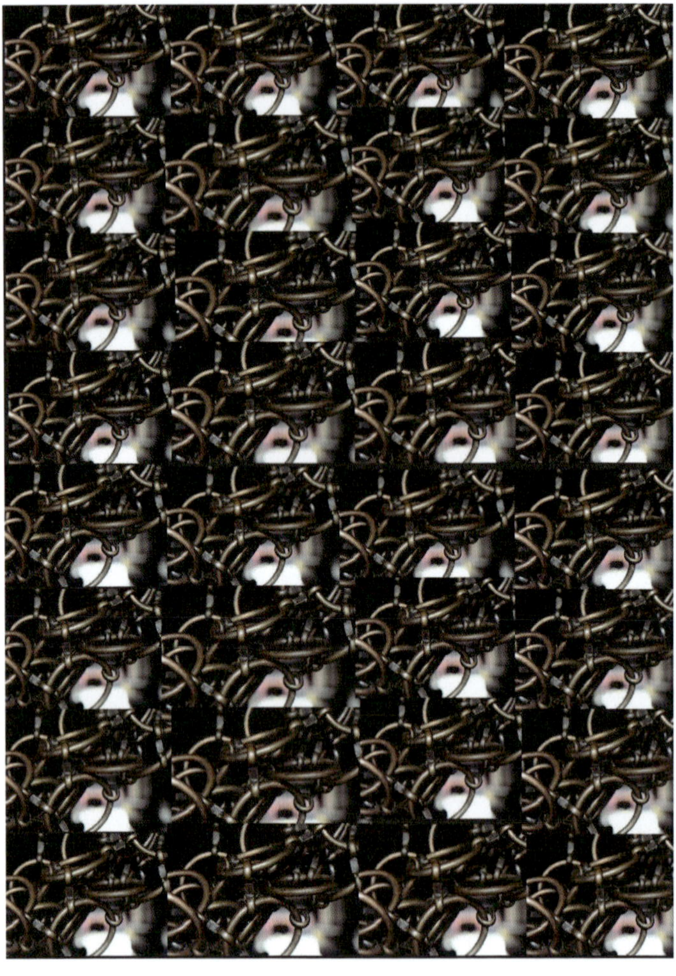

We lock ourselves in

Kora

A footpath to circumnavigating our
Pain
Fear
Moving along with a multitude
All seeking for happiness
With purpose
Towards wisdom and compassion
Moving methodically
Clockwise
The benefits of doing a gymnastic
Accumulating positive karma
Not knowing
I sincerely
With open heart
Walked the kora
Counter clock
Wishing for enlightenment
With no prostration

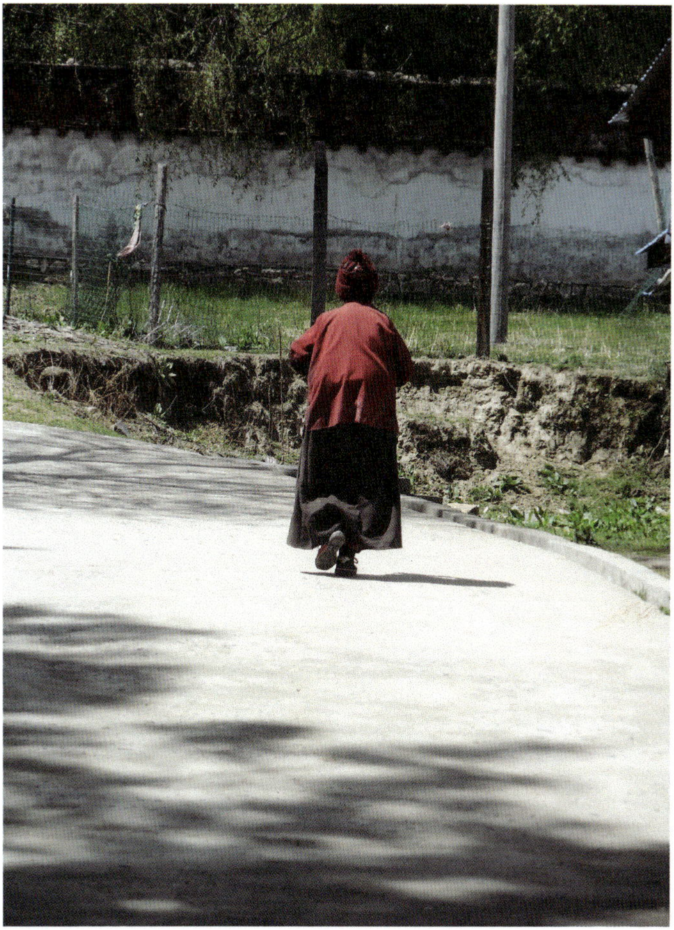

Wheel

You are at the wheel
Steer

Right in that path
Right off the nonsense

Il vento

Le bandiere sventolano
Un arcobaleno in perenne movimento
Come i nostri desideri
di Purezza
di Passione
di Gioia
di Amicizia
E l'intrusa tinta di rosso
Il rosso del sangue versato
E non vendicato
Anche lei sventola al pari dei cavalli alati
Che l'accolgono
Sperando
Che il vento la porti via

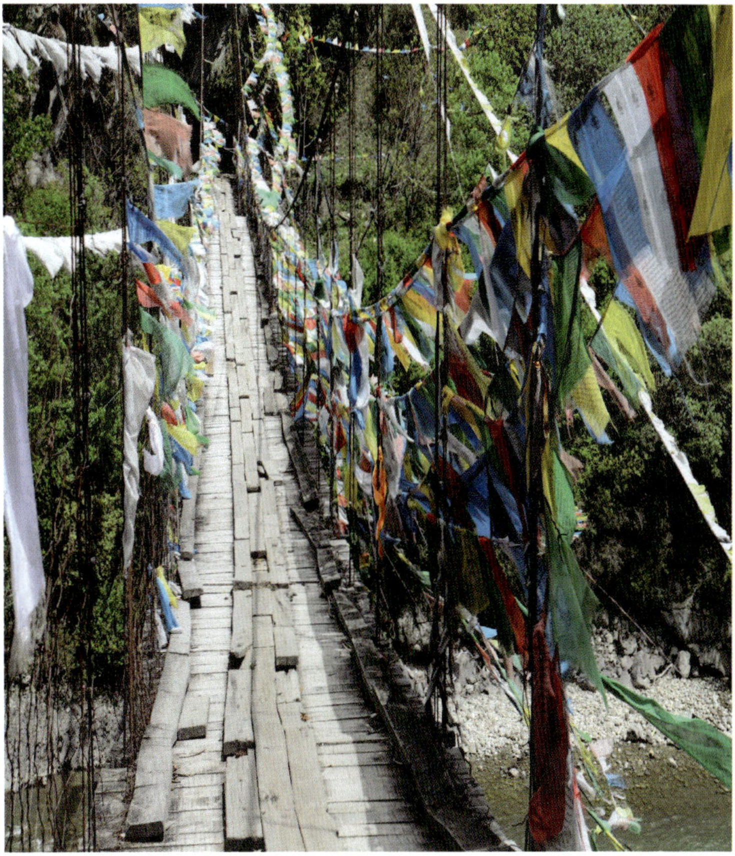

Fateme Banishoeib was born in Italy under the sun of a summer day. In her brings bridged worlds. She is a seeker and a traveler, is many and multitude, deep roads and wild forests. She is passionate about beauty in all its forms, infinitely in love with the heart matters and fond of diversity.

Always with a poem in the hands, in the eyes, in the ears, believing that if we all have four brothers that represent and inhabit the four virtues a person needs to be safe and happy: intelligence, friendship, strength, and poetry...her four brothers are Poetry, Poetry, Poetry and Poetry

> I'm not too articulate when it comes to explaining how I feel about things. But pictures do it for me, they really do. As much as music (and David Bowie).
> **Alessandra Seriacopi**

Printed in Great Britain
by Amazon